Ten Poems
for Winter

ex libris

Candlestick Press

Published by:
Candlestick Press,
Diversity House, 72 Nottingham Road, Arnold, Nottingham UK NG5 6LF
www.candlestickpress.co.uk

Design and typesetting by Craig Twigg

Printed by Ratcliff & Roper Print Group, Nottinghamshire, UK

Selection © Di Slaney and Katharine Towers

Introduction © Di Slaney

Cover illustration © Alexandra Buckle, 2020
www.alexandrabuckle.co.uk

Candlestick Press monogram © Barbara Shaw, 2008

© Candlestick Press, 2020

ISBN 978 1 907598 99 9

Acknowledgements

The poems in this pamphlet are reprinted from the following books, all by
permission of the publishers listed unless stated otherwise. Every effort has
been made to trace the copyright holders of the poems published in this book.
The editors and publisher apologise if any material has been included without
permission or without the appropriate acknowledgement, and would be glad to be
told of anyone who has not been consulted.

Thanks are due to all the copyright holders cited below for their kind permission:

Christine Coates, poem first printed in this pamphlet; Jane Duran, *Breathe,
Now, Breathe* (Enitharmon Editions, 1995); Robert Hayden, *Collected Poems*
(WW Norton, Liveright, 1985); Rhiannon Hooson, poem first printed in this
pamphlet; Christopher James, poem first printed in this pamphlet; Ted Kooser,
Sure Signs (University of Pittsburgh Press, 1980) © 1980 reprinted by permission
of University of Pittsburgh Press; Ruby Robinson, *Every Little Sound* (Liverpool
University Press: Pavilion Poetry Series, 2016); Rob Walton, poem first printed in
this pamphlet; Holly Yuille, poem first printed in this pamphlet.

All permissions cleared courtesy of Swift Permissions
swiftpermissions@gmail.com

Where poets are no longer living, their dates are given.

Contents

Introduction

Poets seem to particularly love winter – the juxtaposition of ice and fire, memories of snowy childhoods, the harsh yet rewarding beauty of the natural world – all provocations for thoughts that may have more time to be committed to paper, now that we're likely to be indoors rather than outside.

So we were spoilt in making our selection for this mini-anthology, particularly as we ran competitions for poems about snow AND winter. Several feature in this pamphlet – Rob Walton's fantastic single sentence riff on *In the Bleak Midwinter* opens the selection, and Holly Yuille (a poet with a name for winter, surely) conjures up a grittily realistic Christmas party in a disco tent with "pounding Northern Soul".

The "small perfections" of nature illuminate Rhiannon Hooson's quietly moving walk across a snowy field in 'The Ragged Kingdom', just three poems away from John Clare's 'Winter Fields' of "mire and sludge" where shepherds and their dogs labour in all weathers. This contrast of beauty and danger features in Christopher James' lyric poem 'Chasing the Light', where a family of hunters skates along "the edge of winter" to a promise of meeting with the light, and a shimmering maternal spirit.

Then we have a tortoise hibernating in a fridge courtesy of Ruby Robinson, and the making of the perfect 'Snow Pudding' by Jane Duran. Christine Coates brings us poignantly into present focus with the emotionally loaded 'January Skype July'.

And whether it's the children "stiffened by winter" in Ted Kooser's 'Late February' or Robert Hayden's suffering, angry father "with cracked hands" in 'Those Winter Sundays', people live and struggle and love their way through all these winter poems to survive till the warmth of spring. We hope you'll read these poems somewhere safe and cosy, and meet us there.

Di Slaney

Bleakmid

We sing *In the Bleak Midwinter* as we pull
cords, tightening hoodies and raincoats
over burning cold faces and I remember
an expectant friend named Winter and a joke
about calling the child Bleakmid
and I hope the girl, graced with a brighter name
builds close-knit snow families and finds dark shining
coal for the eyes and knows that like love
in December it can warm us and I hope
the girl can melt snow and see freezing's
icy beauty and fragility
and I hope she has someone to light scarlet fires
and raise amber toasts
to keep all her winters warm

Rob Walton

Winter

We keep the tortoise in the fridge through the winter. We buy our shopping from the corner shop on the way home from work, as and when we need it. We dry our washing on radiators. We pick chillies from the medusa chilli plant on the kitchen windowsill. We listen to the same CD over & over for days, weeks at a time. We eat chilli most nights. We take it in turns to wash up. We talk a fair bit with the curtains closed. We talk about your ex-lovers. We talk about chelonian hibernation and substrates. We sometimes talk about sphagnum moss. We check the tortoise, although we don't really know what it is we are checking. You put an extra blanket on our bed. We sleep.

Ruby Robinson

Now

Now is the winter of our disco tent.
It was closed for the summer
but they've fixed the air conditioning
and we can climb inside
with our fluffy Russian hats and our mittens.

The girls in short skirts can huddle together
with corned beef legs
clutching their bruised arms and their cigarettes.

We can dance to the lascivious pleasing of a lute
underneath the frozen mirrorball,
and the one that the light touches is the one that you love,
the ones that the light touches are the ones that you love.

The son and heir over there
will stand on his own and leave on his own,
so lame and unfashionable
that dogs bark at him and his out of date platform shoes.

We can crack stalactites of ice into our vodka
and taste the bitter rain water melting into our drinks,
leaning too close with unfocussed eyes
and spilling drunken prophecies, libels and dreams.

We can huddle in the middle at the end of the dancing
a ragged mountain of limbs, blankets and woolly coats,
our thoughts diving down to a lullaby
of pounding Northern Soul.

Holly Yuille

Snow Pudding

One way is to pour maple syrup
on fresh snow. Find a corner
by the house that the wind misses.
Do not dream of it but do it –
syrup that drifts from the maple,
your sticky mittens.

Or sprinkle gelatine over water,
add sugar, lemon. Heat gently.
It seems so effortless,
like the minnows that will appear
in the pond this summer,
so many tourings against rock,

remedies, quickenings,
or the powerful states of shade
under the waterfall.
Beat the egg whites – fold in
to bring the snow that races,
the doe at the window.

In grandmother's kitchen
there is an ooze from the oven dish
with the Atlantic in it,
a hush over it,
an invisible recipe
at the back of the cookbook –

how to prepare snow
when it is really taking you sideways
out of control –
past the side of the house
past the lost barn, journeying
with the blurred crossings

everywhere the land still rising.
Bring in your black and white branches.
Lay your icy clouds on the table.
The roads are impassable.

Jane Duran

The Ragged Kingdom

Winter levels the landscape to rubble. Each night
water rises all across the fields and the snow there
rots once more to rind, a skin of ice

across each ploughed furrow that seems soluble
to its own shadow, granular with time.
The tarn's mouth is stopped with ice

but between intersecting flurries are small perfections:
three red berries on the snowy bank, and a path
between the elders like a dance. And when I turn back

to where my own footsteps darken the blanked out field, this:
the tracks of some animal approaching my own,
but stopping short, perhaps watching for a moment,
then turning away and skimming its own path
back towards the wood.

Rhiannon Hooson

Those Winter Sundays

Sundays too my father got up early
and put his clothes on in the blueblack cold,
then with cracked hands that ached
from labor in the weekday weather made
banked fires blaze. No one ever thanked him.

I'd wake and hear the cold splintering, breaking.
When the rooms were warm, he'd call,
and slowly I would rise and dress,
fearing the chronic angers of that house,

Speaking indifferently to him,
who had driven out the cold
and polished my good shoes as well.
What did I know, what did I know
of love's austere and lonely offices?

Robert Hayden

Chasing the Light

We made ourselves skates of bone
to glide along the edge of winter.
The sky was a fleece of white.
My father cut us each a branch of ash
to steady ourselves against the ice.
Tonight, he said, *we follow the river*
to take us to the light. Do not delay,
for Skadi the hunter, kin of Njorer,
kin of Odin will be at our heels.

Listen and you will hear her arrows
shiver through the trees. Lose your way,
and throw these seeds to the wind.
I will see where the lapwings flock.
Around my shoulders hung the pelt
of a polar fox; the forest smelt
of smoke and snow and midnight.
Our breath melted like ghosts.
My brother, Haken, took the lead.

He wore wolfskin and a heavy heart.
The bones bore us swiftly on.
I saw a kite printed on the moon
while the fish darted beneath the ice.
Then before me: a wolf bigger than a man,
eyes like cold amber. Its paws clawed
on the ice; its jaws mauled the air.
My father cried: *Stand your ground, Ylva,*
raise your branch and do not show your fear.

I felt the weight of snow on the Earth,
closed my eyes and he was gone.
We raced on, skimming the ice-road,
water gushing beneath our feet,
until my father slowed and pointed up
at the sky and the light he had promised.
I watched my mother's spirit melt
and shimmer; her skirts of sapphire,
as she danced with the emerald phantoms.

Christopher James

January Skype July

Our hands touching – the thin foil between us
a third skin, it gives a little under pressure
as when we press our palms together.
Through a window I climb where snow lies on the lawn
and you say 'Come and see' and open the door
to the garden and your mum comes with your coat and boots.
You hold handfuls of snow to my face, say
'You can eat it', your eyes laughing as you gulp it down
and show me red berries on the naked tree, footprints on the icy track.
Then you ride your bicycle and pedal fast and out of sight.
Your mum puts her face into my window
until you're back – red-cheeked and white-flaked hair.
Your dad says to come in for dinner.
I lean forward but I can't smell the juicy chops
so I turn my window to the sky and show you my evening
the sun casting the mountain orange and you stop and point
at the fire for our barbecue and the pool of blue water.
I ask if you can imagine swimming now –
of course you can. You're six and your world stretches and you come
'See I'm climbing through the window' –
and your eyes are so close I can see into your pupil – a membrane away –
you open your mouth wide, I see your little epiglottis laughing in its
                                                                    pink cavern.
Your dad says to stop but I want to climb into that cave.
Now you're playing Danish songs, showing me the tree and decorations
while I'm here, tears falling on the screen,
raindrops on window panes.

Christine Coates

Winter Fields

O for a pleasant book to cheat the sway
Of winter – where rich mirth with hearty laugh
Listens and rubs his legs on corner seat
For fields are mire and sludge – and badly off
Are those who on their pudgy paths delay
There striding shepherd seeking driest way
Fearing nights wetshod feet and hacking cough
That keeps him waken till the peep of day
Goes shouldering onward and with ready hook
Progs oft to ford the sloughs that nearly meet
Across the lands – croodling and thin to view
His loath dog follows – stops and quakes and looks
For better roads – till whistled to pursue
Then on with frequent jump he hirkles through

John Clare

Late February

The first warm day,
and by mid-afternoon
the snow is no more
than a washing
strewn over the yards,
the bedding rolled in knots
and leaking water,
the white shirts lying
under the evergreens.
Through the heaviest drifts
rise autumn's fallen
bicycles, small carnivals
of paint and chrome,
the Octopus
and Tilt-A-Whirl
beginning to turn
in the sun. Now children,
stiffened by winter
and dressed, somehow,
like old men, mutter
and bend to the work
of building dams.
But such a spring is brief;
by five o'clock
the chill of sundown,
darkness, the blue TVs
flashing like storms
in the picture windows,
the yards gone gray,
the wet dogs barking
at nothing. Far off
across the cornfields
staked for streets and sewers,
the body of a farmer
missing since fall

will show up
in his garden tomorrow,
as unexpected
as a tulip.

Ted Kooser